making an impression

Designing & Creating Artful Stamps

Geninne D. Zlatkis

LARK

Editor: Linda Kopp
Art Director: Kristi Pfeffer
Designers: Amy Sly & Kristi Pfeffer
Illustrator: Geninne D. Zlatkis
Photographer: Geninne D. Zlatkis
Cover Designer: Kristi Pfeffer

An Imprint of Sterling Publishing
387 Park Avenue South
New York, NY 10016

Text, photography, and illustrations © 2012, Geninne D. Zlatkis

ISBN 978-1-4547-0125-5

Library of Congress Cataloging-in-Publication Data

Zlatkis, Geninne.
  Making an impression : designing & creating artful stamps / Geninne D. Zlatkis.
    p. cm.
  Includes index.
  ISBN 978-1-4547-0125-5 (alk. paper)
  1. Rubber stamp printing. 2. Rubber stamp art. I. Title.
  TT867.Z58 2012
  761--dc23
                    2011042356

Distributed in Canada by Sterling Publishing
c/o Canadian Manda Group, 165 Dufferin Street
Toronto, Ontario, Canada M6K 3H6
Distributed in the United Kingdom by GMC Distribution Services
Castle Place, 166 High Street, Lewes, East Sussex, England BN7 1XU
Distributed in Australia by Capricorn Link (Australia) Pty. Ltd.
P.O. Box 704, Windsor, NSW 2756, Australia

For information about custom editions, special sales, and premium
and corporate purchases, please contact Sterling Special Sales at
800-805-5489 or specialsales@sterlingpublishing.com.

Email academic@larkbooks.com for information about desk and examination
copies. The complete policy can be found at larkcrafts.com.

Manufactured in China

6 8 10 9 7 5

larkcrafts.com

Introduction 8

STAMPING BASICS

PROJECTS + IDEAS

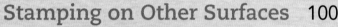

Introduction

I've been passionately curious about how things are made since I was a little girl. I was always fascinated by office supplies like date and number stamps, seals on my passport, and chops on different official documents. When I was a kid, playing teacher wouldn't have been the same without having a stamp to use on all the make-believe tests I had to grade from my dolls.

The first time I ever thought about making my own stamps was a long, long time after my school years. I saw a beautiful wooden tray full of hand-carved wine corks in Gwen Diehn's book, *The Decorated Page*. I was intrigued with the possibility of not only creating my own designs but being able to print them in multiples.

After I purchased a linoleum cutter, a box full of white erasers, and a black ink pad at the local office supply shop, I was instantly hooked. I found I could spend hours at carving, which, to me, was both relaxing and meditative. It made me smile when I remembered that my paternal great-grandfather was a master wood-carver and that he must have also spent hours and hours enjoying this wonderful craft.

Right from the start of writing this book, I knew I wanted it to be a resource as well as an inspiration to all of you who want to learn how to make your own stamps. With that in mind, this book provides you with the basics you'll need to get started. I've included information on tools, materials, techniques, and design. You'll see how easy it is to carve a stamp, build a design using different motifs, and even how to incorporate simple embroidery and sewing techniques into your stamping.

While you'll learn that the tools you need are few, simple, and inexpensive, you'll soon find the design possibilities are endless. I've included 20 projects to get you started. Step-by-step photos will easily lead you through them. I'm hoping that once you make a few, they'll serve as bridges to your imagination to help you create your own.

Throughout this book you'll see photos of the flowers, foliage, wildlife, and architecture of the beautiful area I live in. (If you visit my website, www.geninne.com, you'll see even more examples.) They're my source of inspiration, and may inspire you, too. By sharing these images, I hope you're encouraged to look at the beauty that surrounds you, which, in many cases can be as close as your own backyard. May you find as much joy in this craft as I have!

Geninne D. Zlatkis

Stamping Basics

You may already be an experienced stamper, or you may be a beginner. Either way, you're here because there's something about making an impression that has captured your imagination—if not your full-blown passion. While this book is meant to inspire you, it's also meant to help you as you practice this wonderful craft. Every project begins as an idea, but it's the tools, materials, and techniques wielded by human hands that make the project come to life.

the first cut is the deepest

Start with a simple shape, like a single leaf motif, and then work your way up to more intricate designs. If you've never carved a stamp before, it will take you a little time to get comfortable using the carving tools (see Carving Stamps and Making Impressions on page 18). Make sure you're kind to yourself as you practice, and be prepared to use everything you do as a learning opportunity!

It Starts with an Idea

Deciding what to carve might be the most difficult part of making stamps. I encourage artists to slow down and appreciate the colors and textures of their surroundings. A willingness to observe is all it takes. The more you take time to look around, the easier you'll find it becomes to see the beautiful ideas that are waiting for you in your own backyard.

My main inspiration comes from observing nature on walks with my dog, Turbo. I'm fortunate to live in a part of the world known for its distinct natural beauty. But even in the midst of an urban or suburban landscape, you'd be surprised at what you can find that will inspire your designs. My best advice is to go outside with a camera or a sketchbook. Taking a trip to the park or botanic garden, visiting a flower shop, or even looking at window boxes and trees that line the streets will yield an abundance of ideas to get you started.

I also find that books are a great source of inspiration. Whenever I feel I'm out of ideas, all I have to do is pick up a book with vintage botanical illustrations and I'm instantly inspired. An internet search can also open you to a world of new ideas. You can look at and learn about the flora and fauna of your area, or take a botanist's trip around the world from the comfort of your own home.

Tools and Materials

The tools and materials for stamping are few and inexpensive. You may find
that you already have some of them tucked in among your other craft supplies.
On page 18 you'll find a basic list to get you started. The following
explanations will help familiarize you with what you'll need.

TEMPLATES

You'll find templates to trace on pages 126 to 133 for each of the projects in the book. I also provided 50 additional motifs for you to use. Please feel free to interchange them for the different projects or when making projects of your own design.

CARVING BLOCKS

There are many types of soft rubber carving blocks on the market. The techniques used in this book use a very thick, soft, white rubber block, the same material used in white rubber erasers. I love this type of block because it's so thick that it doesn't need to be mounted on any type backing, and you can easily grab it with your fingers. You can find the carving blocks at your local craft store or on the internet. I don't recommend using linoleum blocks for the projects since you need to use special inks and must use a brayer to apply them.

Soft rubber
carving blocks

TRANSFER MATERIALS

You'll need to transfer the lines of your design onto the rubber block for carving. All it takes is tracing paper, a soft-lead pencil, and a bone folder or small spoon. Trace your design using the soft-lead pencil; a standard No. 2 pencil will do. The softer lead allows the lines to easily transfer to the block when you rub the back of the tracing paper with a bone folder or the back of a small spoon. If you regularly work with paper, you may already have a bone folder in your tool kit.

Soft lead pencils
are my favorite

CUTTING AND CARVING TOOLS

Always have a pair of scissors handy for cutting paper or fabric. You'll also need to have a craft knife or utility cutter for cutting the excess rubber around your stamp. They allow you to make a clean-edged impression and to cut the rubber block into smaller-sized pieces as needed.

linoleum cutters are very sharp! So be careful!

Scissors

Craft knife or utility cutter

For carving, you'll need a tool used for cutting linoleum blocks. One of the most common brands of linoleum cutters, the one I use in this book, comes with a plastic or wooden handle and interchangeable cutting tips that allow you to make a range of lines from thin to thick. Other tools have fixed tips set in individual handles. If you already own a set of linoleum or wood-carving tools you can use the ones you have.

Manufacturers may have different numbering systems to denote the sizing of their cutting tips. In the instructions, I refer to No. 1, No. 2, and No. 5 cutting tips because they're the ones that came with my brand of linoleum cutter. I like to use the fine No. 1 and No. 2 cutters to carve out thin lines and details. I use the wider No. 5 U-shaped cutter to cut away large areas of the stamps that will not be printed. If you already have different carving tools, adjust the instructions to use cutters that will make the lines as described above.

INK

All of the projects in this book were done using pre-inked, acid-free, archival, pigment ink pads. You can easily find them in a range of colors in craft stores or office supply shops. When printing on fabric you must purchase ink pads that are specifically made for textiles. Most fabric inks must be heat set with an iron.

Some pigment ink pads that aren't made for fabric will become permanent if you heat set them with an iron. However, they may not be colorfast when used on fabric that will need to be washed.

If you use the pigment inks this way, test them for colorfastness on a scrap piece of fabric before using them for your project.

Ink pads come in different shapes and sizes. The standard rectangle shape is perfect for most applications. However, the smaller cat's-eye pads come in handy when I want to apply a dab of extra color to a stamp.

← Pigment ink pads in different colors

PRINTING SURFACES

The type of surface you'll be printing on determines the way your impression will look. The smoother the surface, the finer the details will be. Printing on a rough surface will make for a more textured impression (see figure A on page 22). Generally, you should use darker inks on light-colored surfaces and light-colored ink on darker ones, but there's no hard-and-fast rule. Have fun experimenting with your stamps. Matte surfaces are better for rubber stamping than glossy ones, so take that into account when choosing paper or fabric.

Paper

Always choose acid-free, archival paper; it will ensure your creations won't deteriorate with time. But you can stamp just about any type of paper. Watercolor paper in various finishes, smooth to rough, is a versatile heavyweight paper to use. The projects use just about any paper you can imagine. Make sure you have ample scrap paper around, too; you'll use it when testing out your newly carved stamps to make sure the impressions are even.

Fabric

It's important to prepare your fabrics before printing on them by washing, drying, and ironing them beforehand. Since fabrics sometimes shrink a little, it's always best to wash and dry them before sewing any projects. Use fabric inks when stamping on fabric, and follow the manufacturer's instructions for heat setting the ink.

Painted or Other Surfaces

There are few limits to the surfaces you can stamp. The most important rule to remember, however, is to make sure the surface is completely dry and clean of any dust and dirt before making an impression. This holds true whether you're stamping a painted wall, a terracotta pot, or even a rock.

An Eye for Detail

When you want to detail your impressions, you can use a variety of paints and a brush to highlight your designs. On paper and other non-fabric surfaces, fluid acrylics, watercolors, and even iridescent, metallic, or dimensional craft paints will provide the touches you need. When detailing impressions stamped on fabric, keep some fabric paint handy for adding that extra flair.

Take Me Back

I love using paper ephemera in my projects. The little bits you use to flavor your work can evoke a different time and place from Victoriana to Retro. They make wonderful surfaces on which to stamp. Look for old postcards, tags, or bits of vintage wrapping paper. You can find them at flea markets or maybe even at grandma's house. And, there are many shops that sell paper ephemera online, making them only a click away.

GLUE

No mystery here. PVA (polyvinyl acetate) glue, also known as bookbinders glue, will be all you need when you are affixing paper to project. To prevent wrinkles, look for high-quality PVAs made specifically for bookbinding that are sold in art or craft shops.

MISCELLANEOUS TOOLS AND MATERIALS

Embellishments can enhance your stamped designs. Stitchery, beads, charms, and various cording are fun ways to add interest to them.

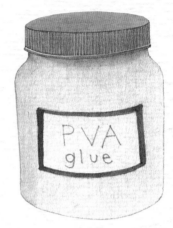

Sewing Machine

A few projects, such as the French Press Cozy (page 84) and the Three Little Birds Pillow (page 96) call for the use of a sewing machine. Neither of them use any fancy techniques and are perfectly suitable for beginners.

↑ PVA glue or white glue

Embroidery Floss and Needle

Stitching adds texture to a stamped design. While you most often think about sewing on fabric, you can stitch on paper as well. Use an embroidery hoop when stitching on fabric for the best results. You'll find a guide to the hand stitches used in the projects on page 29.

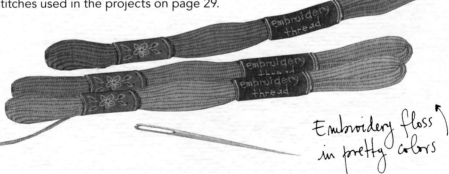

Embroidery floss in pretty colors ↑

Beads and Charms

If you can add stitching to a design, you can also add beads. Sewing small seed beads to a motif is a perfect accent, and a strategically placed charm can add a nice touch.

Cording

Sometimes you just need to wrap it all up. Cording, twine, artificial sinew, or raffia can provide the proper finishing touch.

Techniques

Here is everything you need to know about carving your own stamps and making perfect impressions, techniques for applying basic design principles to your stamping, and hand stitching for added embellishment.

18

CARVING STAMPS AND MAKING IMPRESSIONS

Follow the steps and you won't go wrong! Refer to this section as needed when making any of the individual projects. Allow yourself time to practice. It may take awhile to become totally comfortable with the tools and carving techniques. Once you master these basic skills, you're ready to begin.

What You'll Need

Before you begin, gather your tools and materials. Below is a list of the basic items you'll need to create the projects. The individual project instructions will include any additional tools and materials you might need to complete that particular project.

- Tracing paper
- Soft-lead pencil—a standard No. 2 lead pencil is perfect for this work
- Bone folder or small spoon
- Rubber carving blocks or white rubber erasers
- Linoleum cutter with No. 1, No. 2, and No. 5 cutting tips
- Craft knife or utility cutter
- Ink pads

In General, Here's What You Do

(1) Find an image you would like to use. For inspiration, look at books, magazines, or your own photos or drawings. I've also provided templates for each design used in the projects. Use a piece of the tracing paper and the soft-lead pencil to trace all lines of the image or template (**A**).

(2) Stain the carving block with an ink pad before tracing over it. **Note:** This step is optional—I learned this tip from a Japanese craft book—but I've found it to be incredibly helpful when I get to the carving stage. The colored surface makes it easier to see the areas you've carved. Lay the rubber block on your work surface, and ink it with the ink pad facing down. Use a patting motion on the pad until the block is completely covered with ink. Allow the ink to dry 15 minutes, and then wash it gently under running water using a small amount of pH neutral soap. The surface will be permanently stained and will not smudge. Pat it dry with a paper towel (**B**).

(3) Lay the traced image on top of the carving block with the pencil lines facing down, and hold it in place with one hand. Rub the back of the paper with the bone folder or the back of a small spoon, making sure the paper doesn't move as you rub. Use a firm and steady pressure until all the lines of the image have been transferred onto the carving block. When you're done, hold a corner of the paper in place and lift it slightly to check if the whole design was transferred onto the surface of the block. If not, just lower the paper and rub it again (**C**).

Flip It

When you use tracing paper to transfer an image onto the rubber block, the images will be automatically flipped and the image will be exactly as it is oriented on the template. If you draw directly onto the rubber block, you need to consider that when you carve out your design the image will be reversed like a mirror image. This is especially important to keep in mind when you're carving a stamp that includes text.

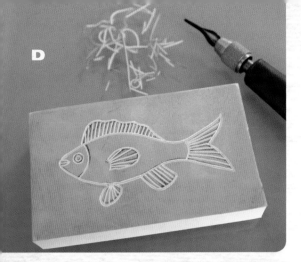

④ Use the linoleum cutter with the No. 1 tip (the thinnest one) to carve out the lines of the design. Do not jab the tip into the block when carving. Keep the cutter at a 30° angle, and make sure the top part of the blade does not sink below the surface of the rubber block. Use this thin tip almost like a pen or pencil, as if you're drawing on the carving block. The cutting tip has a slight curve that you should use as one would use a spoon or little shovel to scoop out the rubber material (**D**).

Be Careful!

Always carve away from yourself, and be mindful that the tips are very sharp. When you need to change the direction in which you are carving, rotate the block so you can continue to carve away from yourself.
Note: I like to put a piece of tracing paper under the carving block, which makes the block easier to slide around.

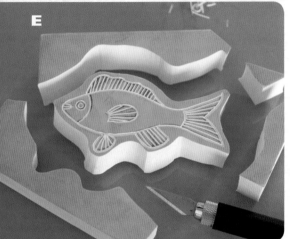

⑤ After you've finished cutting out all the lines of the design, use the craft knife or utility cutter to cut around the outline of the shape. Precision counts! Keeping the lines crisp and clean makes clear impressions. Discard the excess rubber block (**E**).

⑥ Use the linoleum cutter with the wider No. 5 tip to carve around the shape and to clean out the outer edges. Switch back to using the No. 1 tip to clean out all the nooks and crannies (**F**).

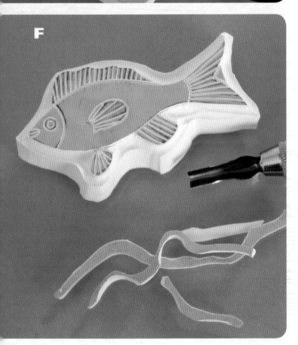

⑦ When you're finished carving, wash your stamp with warm water and pH neutral soap to clean out any crumbs of rubber that may be left behind. Pat the stamp dry, and allow it to air dry for a few minutes before inking.

⑧ To ink stamps, place the stamps faceup on your work surface. With the ink pad facing down, pat the stamp with the pad until it's completely and uniformly covered with ink. *Note:* This is my preferred method for inking larger stamps. For smaller stamps, you can ink them by dabbing them directly on the ink pad.

9. Make a few impressions on a sheet of white scrap paper. Practice pressing the stamp down firmly and with uniform pressure to ensure an even transfer of the design. If there are any parts of the stamp that you forgot to carve out, it will show up at this point, and you can go back and make adjustments (**G**).

10. When you're satisfied with the results of your test prints, clean off your work surface to remove any bits and pieces of dirt or carving debris that can affect the quality of the impressions. Lay your paper faceup, making sure it lies flat. Apply firm and uniform pressure to the stamp to make your impression.

11. You can create a gradient color effect on your stamp. To do so, re-ink your stamp with your primary color, and then dab a little ink from an ink pad of a complementary color along the edges of the stamp. *Note:* In this case, I put the complementary color on the fins and tail of the fish (**H**).

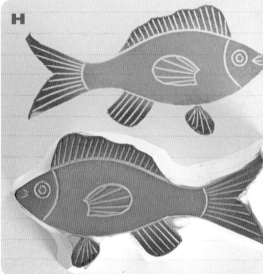

Negative and Positive

There are two ways to carve a stamp; one creates a negative image and the other creates a positive image. To create a negative image, you carve out the lines of the image or template, leaving most of the rubber surface intact, as I did for the fish in this example. **Note:** This is my favorite kind of image because you're able to carve more details. Plus, it's easier to carve since you mostly use the fine No. 1 tip as you would use a pencil for drawing detail. To make the positive image, you carve out most of the block's surface leaving only the outline of the design. You can see the difference between them in the photo right. The stamp for the negative image is in the center. The impression and stamp of the positive image are at the top and bottom. (For more on carving negative and positive stamps, see page 23.)

21

DESIGN

Now that you know the tools and materials you need, and how to actually carve a stamp and make impressions, it's time to cover the basic techniques of design. Because this topic is just about limitless, use the following as beginning tips for expanding your design potential. Ultimately, beauty is in the eye of the artist, meaning you'll have to decide what looks pleasing to you. The only way you'll know what works best for you is to play—and who can resist that invitation?

Texture

The surface you're printing on will determine the texture of the impression. On a rough surface (**A**) you may lose some of the details in your carved design. However, the random unevenness can impart a pleasing texture that makes the impression interesting. When you print on a smooth surface (**B**) the details will be sharper, which, in and of itself, adds texture. If you want a hint of background texture, use the ink pad as a stamp to lightly impress the color directly onto the paper before stamping your motif (**C**).

Repetition

With stamping, realizing that repetition is never dull opens up a world of design possibilities. The most obvious concept is that no two impressions are ever the same, even though at first glance they may look alike. As shown in figure A, the floating bird is stamped at a slightly different angle than the one figure B. This simple variation allows the artist to truly create one-of-a-kind pieces. Some simple ways to vary an impression are trying different angles or orientations of the image when stamping, applying more or less pressure to the stamp, and, of course, changing the colors of ink you use.

Positive and Negative Space

The space you carve out will remain un-inked and show your surface when you make an impression. This is called the negative space. The positive space is the parts of the surface that remain uncarved and will receive the ink to make the impression. In the photo above, you can see how I carved the same leaf motif using both concepts.

Since carving negative and positive space creates two different effects, use it to your advantage. Try using the same motif, carving one as a positive, and the other as a negative, then alternate the stamps to create an interesting visual.

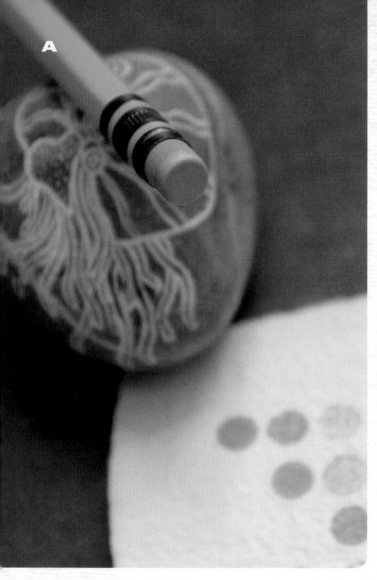

A

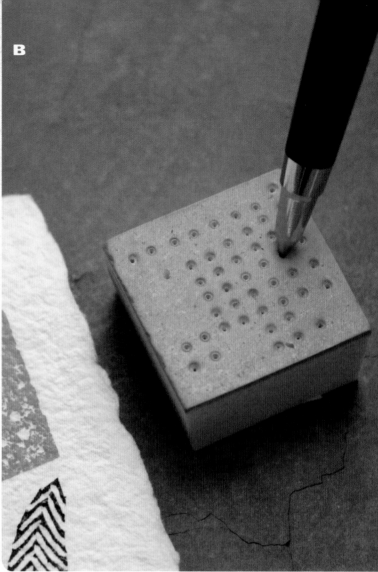

B

Pattern and Rhythm

Pattern can enrich a stamped design when used as a background, or it can stand alone. I often use a pencil eraser to make a dotted pattern (**A**). *Note:* To add some rhythm to the stamped pattern, vary the pressure from light to heavy when making the repeat impressions. I also use the tip of a mechanical pencil to make holes in the surface of a rubber carving block (**B**). Once you've stamped your patterns, you can stamp a motif right over them (**C**).

C

Lines

Never underestimate the power of a line. Whether you overlap them, carve them on the diagonal, or prefer them squiggly or wavy, lines are design elements in their own right (**D**). When carving the lines, experiment by using different size cutting tips. A series of randomly carved short lines on a cutting block makes a great background texture you can use again and again.

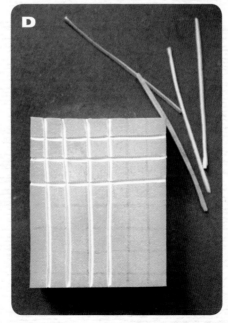

D

A

B

C

D

Composition

Talk about putting it all together! That's exactly what you do when you use separate stamps to create a composed design. The easiest way to begin is to carve stamps of individual motifs that are all related to a theme (**A**). They're pretty when stamped alone, but there's so much more you can do with them (**B**).

Combine two or more stamps to create new designs (**C**). Then have fun seeing what they look like when stamped (**D**). If you want to use a single motif stamp, try stamping it alternately upside down for an interesting variation (**E**). You don't have to limit yourself to stamping side by side. You can stack motifs when you want your designs to go vertical (**F**). The key is to play with the stamps until you find a design that is exactly what you want.

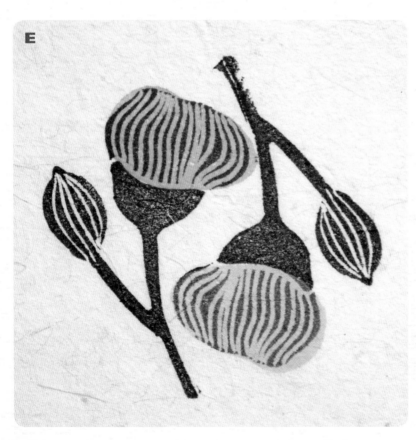

Color

Color as a design element? Absolutely! You can see the potential for this in figure **A**, and all I did was add a second color. *Note:* You don't have to reink a stamp when you want to use more than one color. An easy way to do this is to cut a blank stamp in the shape of choice. In figure **B**, you can see that I cut out a separate leaf shape. After stamping my design in one color, I inked the shape in a contrasting color and stamped over the matching area of the impression to create a second color. Try different color combinations to convey mood, time, or place. Before you know it, you may have developed a signature palette that you alone are known for.

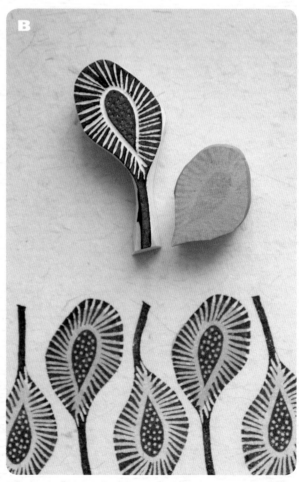

HAND STITCHES

I love combining embroidery with stamped impressions whether they're on paper or fabric. To make the projects, all you'll need are a few basic decorative stitches. I've also included the slip stitch, since you'll use it to attach the pocket to the Embroidered Cactus Tote (page 80) and to close the opening on the Bird Brooch (page 88). If you embroider, I encourage you to creatively use the stitches you know to embellish your impressions any way you like.

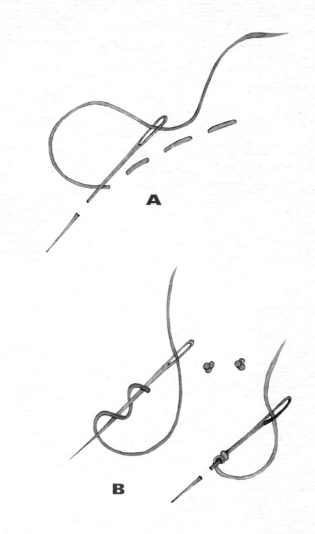

A

Straight Stitch and Running Stitch

Weave the needle through the fabric at evenly spaced intervals (**A**). Several straight stitches in a row are called running stitches.

French Knot

This little knot will add interest and texture to your stamped designs (**B**).

B

Slip Stitch

Knot the end of the thread to anchor it in the fabric. Take a small stitch through the fold, pulling the needle through. In the other side of the seam, insert the needle directly opposite the stitch you just made, and take a stitch through the fold (**C**). Repeat.

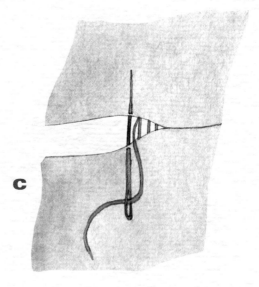

C

inspiration

Go for a walk outside with open eyes and a
camera or sketchbook. You'll unequivocally
find inspiration when you start to take notice
of the natural world around you. Keep an
eye out for interesting shapes, structures,
patterns, and color combinations. Whether
you live in the city or in the country, a good
long walk will bring out your creativity.

STAMPING on paper

eraser stamps

Soft white erasers are easy to find and easy to carve. Their small dimensions allow you to create petite motifs you can use again and again. Stamp your impressions on blank stickers, then use them when sealing envelopes or decorating a wrapped gift.

what you'll need

- Tracing paper
- Soft-lead pencil
- Bone folder or small spoon
- White rubber erasers
- Linoleum cutter with No. 1 and No. 5 tips
- Craft knife or utility cutter
- Ink pads in colors of choice
- Sheets of blank round stickers in different sizes

what you do

① Use the templates on page 126. Trace a design using the soft-lead pencil, and then use the bone folder or small spoon to transfer the image onto the eraser (page 19). *Tip:* Sketching from nature inspires me and can inspire you (**A**). Try creating your own designs—all it takes is a little time, some paper, and a pencil.

② Carve the stamp from the rubber eraser using the linoleum cutter. *Note:* You'll be carving out all the white spaces. Use your cutter as if it were a drawing tool to make all the fine lines. Once you've carved the stamp, give it a light wash with warm water and a pH neutral soap, and let it air dry.

A

③ Test the stamp on a piece of scrap paper first. Practice using uniform and firm pressure to make sure the impression is even. Ink the stamp by dabbing it gently on the ink pad, and stamp it on scrap paper.

TIP: Use different colored ink pads to stamp your designs onto the blank stickers, and let them dry completely before use.

gift tags

If you love giving gifts as much as I do, you can never have enough tags. In fact, I've gotten so used to using tags that a prettily wrapped package looks incomplete without one.

what you'll need

- Tracing paper
- Soft-lead pencil
- Bone folder or small spoon
- Rubber carving block or white rubber erasers
- Linoleum cutter with No. 1 and No. 5 tips
- Craft knife or utility cutter
- Ink pads in colors of choice
- Blank tags in a variety of shapes and sizes, or an assortment of decorative paper

what you do

① Use the template on page 126. Trace a design using the soft-lead pencil, and then use the bone folder or small spoon to transfer the image onto the rubber carving block or eraser (page 19).

② Carve the stamp from the rubber carving block or eraser using the linoleum cutter. Use your cutter as if it were a drawing tool to make all the fine lines. Once you've carved the stamp, give it a light wash with warm water and a pH neutral soap, and let it air dry.

③ Test the stamp on a piece of scrap paper first. Practice using uniform and firm pressure to make sure the impression is even. Ink the stamp by dabbing it gently on the ink pad, and stamp it on scrap paper.

④ Use different colored ink pads to stamp your designs onto the blank tags, and let them dry completely before use (**A**).

TIP: There are many shapes and sizes of blank tags on the market. You can also recycle all sorts of paper like newsprint, cereal boxes, and wrapping paper to make your own—just cut a tag shape from your paper of choice, and make the hole with a hole punch. I have a great die-cut punch in the shape of a typical tag.

TAGS

stationery

Despite living in the age of texts, tweets, and e-mail, the art of the handwritten letter is alive and well. You'll find that nothing enhances a personal note more than lovely stamped stationery.

what you'll need

- Tracing paper
- Soft-lead pencil
- Bone folder or small spoon

- Rubber carving blocks
- Linoleum cutter with No. 1 and No. 5 tips
- Craft knife or utility cutter

- Ink pads in colors of choice
- Variety of stationery, including letterhead paper, envelopes, and cards

what you do

(1) Use the template on page 128. Trace the flower using the soft-lead pencil, and then trace the center of the flower separately (**A**). Use the bone folder or small spoon to transfer the images onto the rubber carving blocks (page 19).

(2) Carve the stamps from the blocks using the linoleum cutter. Use your carving tool as if it were a drawing tool to make all the fine lines. Once you've carved the stamps, give them a light wash with warm water and a pH neutral soap, and let them air dry.

(3) Test the stamp on a piece of scrap paper first. Practice using uniform and firm pressure to make sure the impression is even. With bigger stamps, I like to place the stamp right side up on the table and ink it by dabbing the ink pad evenly onto the surface.

(4) If you want to make a partial impression of your flower stamp, place the piece of paper you want to stamp on a bigger sheet of scrap paper. Ink your stamp, and make the impression by placing the stamp just partly on top of your stationery piece.

(5) You can use the small round stamp by itself to create a pattern.

A

TIP: The real fun of stamping comes from just playing around. Once you've carved your stamps, try using different color combinations, partial imprints, or smaller motifs to create new designs.

BOTSWANA

African Hoopoe

FIRST CLASS MAIL

bookplate

This has got to be the most perfect gift for all the bookworms on your list. Any reader will appreciate having a special bookplate when adding volumes to his or her library. Remember to leave some blank space on the impression for a personalized inscription.

what you'll need

- Tracing paper
- Soft-lead pencil
- Bone folder or small spoon
- Rubber carving block

- Linoleum cutter with No. 1 and No. 5 tips
- Craft knife or utility cutter
- Ink pads in black and dark brown

- Acid-free paper with a smooth surface in a variety of colors
- PVA glue

what you do

1. Use the template on page 126. Trace the design using the soft-lead pencil, and then use the bone folder or small spoon to transfer the image onto the rubber carving block (page 19).

2. Carve the stamp from the rubber carving block using the linoleum cutter. Use your carving tool as if it were a drawing tool to make all the fine lines. Once you've carved the stamp, give it a light wash with warm water and a pH neutral soap, and let it air dry (**A**).

3. Test the stamp on a piece of scrap paper first. Practice using uniform and firm pressure to make sure the impression is even. With bigger stamps, I like to place the stamp right side up on the table and ink it by dabbing the ink pad evenly onto the surface.

EX LIBRIS

Emmme D. Zlatkis

ND FAUNA FROM THE COURT
HE EMPEROR RUDOLF II

CALLIGRAPHY FROM THE COURT OF
THE EMPEROR RUDOLF II

·EX LIBRIS·

LIBRIS

B

④ Cut the acid-free paper to size. *Tip:* You may find it helpful to place the carving block on the book to determine how much of a border you want around the design (**B**).

⑤ Make a few impressions of the bookplate on the cut acid-free paper using the black or dark brown ink. Let the ink dry completely.

⑥ Use the PVA glue to affix the bookplate to the inside cover of your book, and write your name on the space below the birdie.

TIP: The beauty of stamping is that you can use the design as many times as you want, which is perfect when you need to make gifts for a lot of people. Stamp multiple copies of the bookplate, and then make a little envelope to go with each one.

wrapping paper

When it's time to wrap it all up, a few stamps in different shapes and sizes will provide infinite design possibilities for making your own wrapping paper. Pick a theme and go from there. I chose mushrooms for this project, but you can choose any theme, such as birds, flowers, or leaves.

what you'll need

- Tracing paper
- Soft-lead pencil
- Bone folder or small spoon
- Rubber carving blocks

- Linoleum cutter with No. 1 and No. 5 tips
- Craft knife or utility cutter
- Ink pad in white
- Solid-color paper in colors of choice

- Decorative paper in a contrasting solid color
- Jute twine
- Stamped gift tags

what you do

① Use the templates on page 128. Trace the mushroom shapes using the soft-lead pencil. Use the bone folder or small spoon to transfer the images onto the rubber carving blocks (page 19).

② Carve the stamps. For a clean impression, use the craft or utility knife to cut any excess rubber from the edge of each stamp. Once you've carved the stamps, give them a light wash with warm water and a pH neutral soap, and let it air dry.

③ Test the stamp on a piece of scrap paper first. Practice using uniform and firm pressure to make sure the impression is even. With bigger stamps, I like to place the stamp right side up on the table and ink it by dabbing the ink pad evenly onto the surface (**A**).

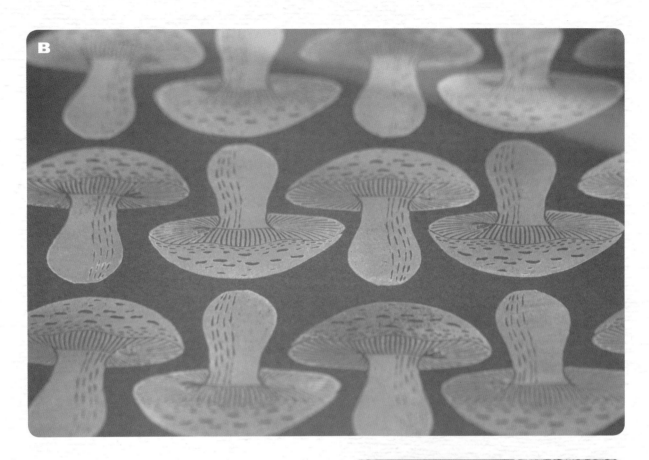

④ Stamp the pattern on a sheet of the solid-color paper. Make one design using the larger mushroom stamp only, reinking as needed. Allow to dry (**B**).

⑤ Create a different pattern on another sheet of paper by stamping the larger mushroom first, and then filling in the gaps using the smaller mushroom stamps. Allow to dry (**C**).

⑥ Wrap your gift with your stamped paper. Decorate one with a strip of the contrasting colored paper if desired. Finish the wrapping with jute twine and a stamped tag (**D**).

I LOVE YOU

TIP: A stamped tag is the perfect way to finish off your beautifully wrapped package. Once you make the stamps for the tags you can stamp on demand, using colors and themes that coordinate with your wrapping paper.

D

photo frame

Use these stamped frames to hold photos or artwork. You can purchase precut mats, or make your own using vintage postcards, paper ephemera, heavyweight decorative papers, or black cardboard.

what you'll need

- Tracing paper
- Soft-lead pencil
- Bone folder or small spoon
- Rubber carving blocks or white rubber erasers

- Linoleum cutter with No. 1 and No. 5 tips
- Craft knife or utility cutter
- Ink pads in colors of choice
- Precut mats, paper ephemera, heavyweight

decorative paper, or black cardboard
- Vintage ephemera (optional)
- Corner rounding punch (optional)

what you do

① Use the templates on page 127. Trace the designs using the soft-lead pencil, and then use the bone folder or small spoon to transfer the images onto the rubber carving block or individual erasers (page 19) (**A**).

② Carve the stamps from the rubber carving block or erasers using the linoleum cutter. *Note:* You can carve several stamps on a larger rubber block and separate them after carving so you can interchange them to make different patterns on different frames. Once you've carved the stamps, give them a light wash with warm water and a pH neutral soap, and let them air dry.

③ Ink the stamps and practice making the impressions on a piece of scrap paper before stamping the frames. Use the corner border to

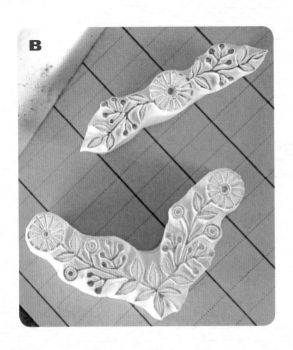

stamp the design in the corners of your mat (**B**), and then use the other stamps to fill out the designs all around. *Tip:* Use white ink if you use a black mat.

④ When stamping around an oval, you can slightly bend the stamp to align to the edge of the opening. **Note:** If you're going to cut an oval opening, use the oval-shaped template.

⑤ Sometimes it's fun to decorate the stamped frame with vintage ephemera. You can also use a corner rounding punch for a more finished look if you're going to use the photo frame in a scrapbook.

TIP: When making your own frames, make sure you cut out the opening 1/4 inch (6 mm) smaller than the size of your image, and then make the border any size you like.

stamped heart wall art

If you're anything like me, you'll find carving stamps so enjoyable that you'll have quite a nice collection of them in no time. Gather them up and stamp your own unique piece of wall art. I made this heart motif using the stamps from the projects in this book.

what you'll need

- Kraft or construction paper, one 12 x 16-inch (30.5 x 40.6 cm) sheet
- Soft-lead pencil
- Scissors
- Watercolor paper with a smooth surface
- Several of the rubber stamps from this book
- Ink pads in colors of choice

what you do

① Make your own heart-shaped template. Fold the piece of kraft or construction paper in half. Use the pencil to draw half a heart, and then cut along the line using the scissors. Unfold the heart shape.

② Center the heart template on the watercolor paper, and trace around it. Use a light hand to make a very thin, nearly invisible line (**A**).

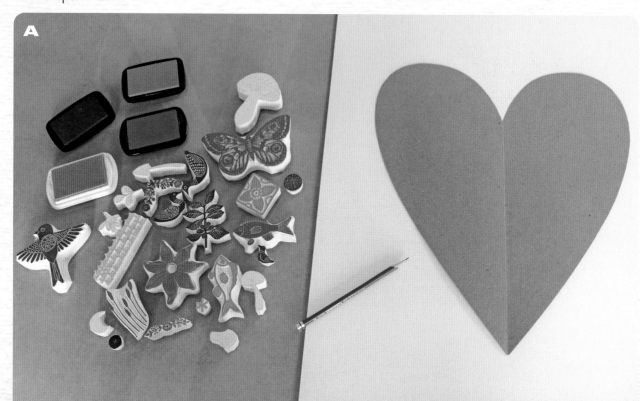

A

(3) Use the stamps and ink pads to fill in the heart shape. *Note:* I stamped the butterfly in the top center of the heart and then used other stamps along the edges before filling in toward the center. Use the smallest stamps to fill in any gaps. Alternating ink colors will create a balanced overall effect. Allow to dry (**B**).

(4) Frame your work of art, and hang it on the wall for all to enjoy.

TIP: You can also make themed wall art. Start with a shape of your choice, then stamp with coordinating impressions. A simple dog or cat shape filled with respectively themed stamps makes a great gift for pet lovers. What about flowers or birds for gardeners? Let your imagination roam.

accordion journal

I think journaling and stamping go hand in hand. Just the right impression can illustrate an emotion or mood, an observation, or a fleeting thought. This easy accordion-fold journal is the perfect way to record and hold your memories.

what you'll need

- Tracing paper
- Soft-lead pencil
- Bone folder or small spoon
- Rubber carving block
- Linoleum cutter with No. 1 and No. 5 tips
- Craft knife or utility cutter
- Ink pad in a color of choice

- Watercolor paper, one 2-inch (5 cm) square
- 1 sheet of handmade paper in a color of your choice
- Inexpensive flat brush
- PVA glue
- Book board, two 5-inch (12.7 cm) squares

- Long strip of paper cut 5 inches (12.7 cm) wide
- Natural twine, two 20-inch-long (50.8 cm) pieces
- Handmade paper, two 5-inch (12.7 cm) squares
- Ceramic or metal charm of choice (optional)

what you do

① Use the template on page 126. Trace the design using the soft-lead pencil, and then use the bone folder or small spoon to transfer the image onto the rubber carving block (page 19) (**A**).

② Carve the stamp from the rubber carving block using the linoleum cutter (**B**). Once you've carved the stamp, give it a light wash with warm water and a pH neutral soap, and let it air dry.

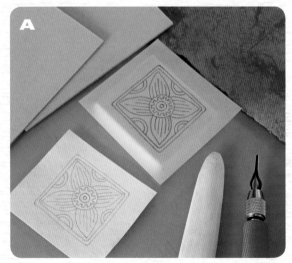

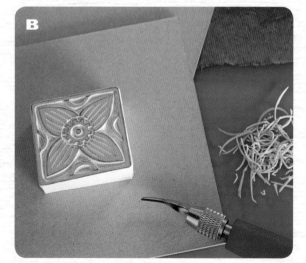

3 Ink the stamp in the color of choice. Make an impression on the 2-inch (5 cm) square of watercolor paper (**C**). Set aside.

4 Place the sheet of handmade paper with its wrong side facing up onto a clean, flat surface. Use the inexpensive flat brush to apply the PVA glue onto one side of each of the book board squares (**D**).

5 Place the book board pieces, glue side down, on the handmade paper, leaving a 1-inch (2.5 cm) border all around (**E**).

6 Use a pair of sharp scissors or a very sharp craft or utility knife to cut out the covers, keeping the 1-inch (2.5 cm) border around each of the pasted book boards. Trim the paper at each corner on the diagonal (**F**).

7 Brush glue evenly onto the flaps of paper (**G**), fold them in, and press with a bone folder or spoon to smooth (**H**).

8 Fold each end of the long strip of paper in 2 inches (5 cm) (**I**). Then use the accordion fold to make each page 5 inches (12.7 cm) square (**J**).

TIP! Use the journal to record all the stamps. Remember to date each page.

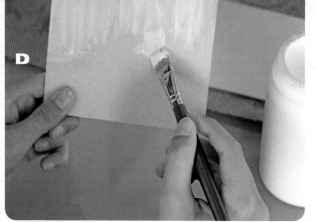

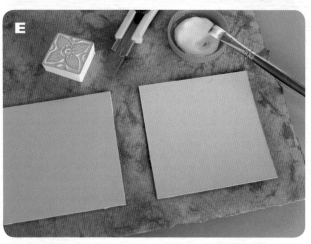

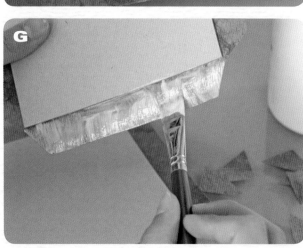

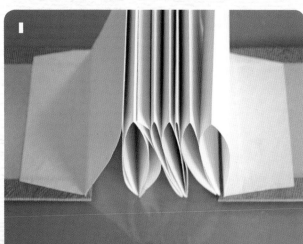

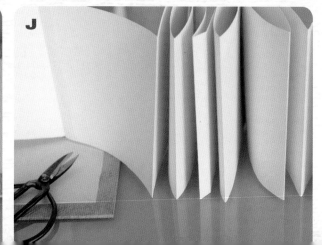

(9) Glue the end flaps of the accordion-folded booklet onto each of the covers.

(10) Center a piece of the natural twine horizontally on each of the covers, and glue in place (**K**). Glue one of the 5-inch (12.7 cm) squares of the handmade paper onto the inside of each cover, covering both the end flap and the twine.

(11) Glue the stamped piece of watercolor paper made in step 3 to the center of the journal cover. Wrap the strings around the journal to close. If you'd like, attach a ceramic or metal charm to the string to enhance the stamped design (**L**).

embroidered cards

Embroidery on cards opens up a whole world of textural possibilities. The raised effect allows design elements to leap off the page, and just a little bit can go a long way. The options are limitless as embroidery floss is available in every conceivable color, and some specialty floss even has metallic or glow-in-the-dark fibers—perfect for holiday cards!

what you'll need

- Tracing paper
- Soft-lead pencil
- Bone folder or small spoon
- Rubber carving block
- Linoleum cutter with No. 1 and No. 5 tips

- Craft knife or utility cutter
- Ink pads in colors of choice
- Scrap paper
- Vintage book pages
- PVA glue
- Premade cards
- Sewing machine (optional)

- Small piece of thin cardboard (a cereal box will work)
- Piece of foam core or corrugated cardboard
- Embroidery needle
- Embroidery floss in colors of choice

what you do

① Use the template on page 127. Trace the little town using the soft-lead pencil (**A**). Use the bone folder or small spoon to transfer the image onto the rubber carving block (page 19).

② Carve the stamp from the block using the linoleum cutter. Use the No. 1 tip, the thinnest one, to carve out the lines. Once you've carved the stamp, give it a light wash with warm water and a pH neutral soap, and let it air dry.

③ Test out the stamp on a scrap piece of paper. Practice using uniform and firm pressure to make sure the impression is even.

④ Ink the stamp and press it onto a vintage book page using uniform pressure to make sure the whole design gets transferred onto the paper (**B**). With bigger stamps, I like to place the stamp right side up on the table and ink it by dabbing the ink pad evenly on the surface. Cut the impression from the paper, leaving a ½-inch (1.3 cm) border all around.

⑤ Use the PVA glue to attach the impression to the front of the premade card. You can also use your sewing machine to attach it (**C**). *Note:* For this project, I used my sewing machine and stitched a line around the perimeter of the impression.

⑥ Make a pattern for the sewing holes. Draw the motif you will embroider on the small piece of cardboard. Lay it on the corrugated cardboard or foam core, and use the embroidery needle to punch the sewing holes into and through it.

⑦ Open the card and lay the front on the corrugated cardboard or foam core. Position the punched pattern on the impression (**D**). Use the embroidery needle to punch the sewing holes into and through the card. Continue repositioning the pattern on the card to punch all holes as necessary.

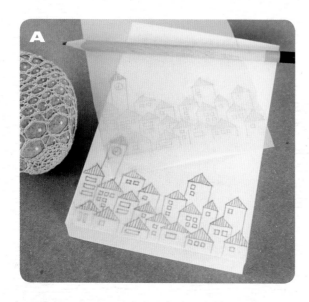

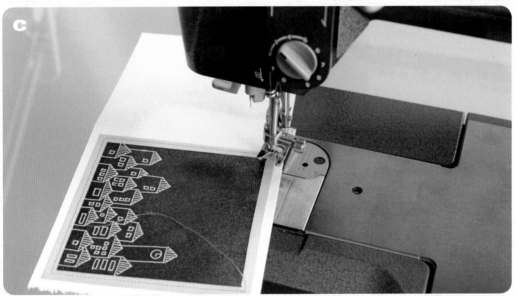

⑧ Use the embroidery floss and embroidery needle to sew through the holes to create the embroidered motifs (**E**).

⑨ Punch sewing holes around the edges of the impression (**F**).

⑩ Use embroidery floss and a needle to sew a stitched frame around the impression (**G**).

TIP: Try different motifs for embellishing the sky. Stars, clouds, rain, sun, or birds are some of the most popular choices. Use dark ink on the stamp for a night or stormy sky and brighter colors when you want a daylight effect.

butterfly vintage postcard

This butterfly looks as if it came straight out of a Victorian collector's specimen box. After stamping, you hand color the impression with watercolors. Researching a butterfly book will provide ample inspiration when choosing which colors to use.

what you'll need

- Tracing paper
- Soft-lead pencil
- Bone folder or small spoon
- Rubber carving block
- Linoleum cutter with No. 1 and No. 5 tips
- Craft knife or utility cutter
- Ink pads in black or dark brown
- Watercolor paper with a smooth surface
- Watercolors in colors of your choice
- Medium round brush
- Vintage postmarked postcards
- PVA glue

what you do

① Use the template on page 127. Trace the design using the soft-lead pencil, and then use the bone folder or small spoon to transfer the image onto the rubber carving block (page 19) (**A**).

② Carve the stamp from the rubber carving block using the linoleum cutter. *Tip:* When carving, remember to carve out the white spaces, leaving the black lines of the motif. Once you've

carved the stamp, give it a light wash with warm water and a pH neutral soap, and let it air dry (**B**).

3 Test the stamp on a piece of scrap paper first. Practice using uniform and firm pressure to make sure the impression is even. With bigger stamps, I like to place the stamp right side up on the table and ink it by dabbing the ink pad evenly on the surface.

4 Ink the stamp with black or dark brown ink, and then make an impression of the butterfly on the watercolor paper. Allow the ink to dry completely (**C**).

5 Use the watercolors and the medium round brush to color all the white spaces of the butterfly motif. Play around with the colors, allowing each to dry before applying a new one. Stamp a few butterflies and color each one differently. You may even want to leave reality behind and color a few using purely fantastical colors (**D**).

6 To create the 3-D effect, cut out one of your finished butterflies and fold both wings along the butterfly's body. Glue the underside of the butterfly's body to a vintage postcard (**E**).

TIP: You can also mount your butterfly in a specimen box. Paint a recycled box, and pin the butterfly inside. (Small cardboard gift boxes with clear covers work best.) Don't forget to make a little label with a make-believe scientific name on it to stick to the cover.

garden journal

A garden journal helps me keep track of the most mundane chores. But I find that it's also compost for my soul. The thoughts I record during the growing months keep me warm all winter long.

what you'll need

- Tracing paper
- Soft-lead pencil
- Bone folder or small spoon
- Rubber carving blocks or small white rubber erasers

- Linoleum cutter with No. 1 and No. 5 tips
- Craft knife or utility cutter
- Small piece of watercolor paper

- Hand-bound journal
- Metal ruler
- Scrap paper
- Ink pads in different colors
- PVA glue

what you do

① Use the templates on page 132. Trace all the pots and plants using the soft-lead pencil. Use the bone folder or small spoon to transfer the images onto the rubber carving blocks or small white rubber erasers (page 19) (**A**).

② Carve the stamps. For a clean impression, use the craft or utility knife to cut any excess rubber from the edge of each stamp. Carve the pots separately from the plants so you can interchange them to create different combinations. Once you've

A

carved the stamps, give them a light wash with warm water and a pH neutral soap, and let them air dry (**B**).

(3) Cut a 2-inch (5 cm) square from the watercolor paper. Position the square where you want it on the cover of the hand-bound journal, and lightly trace around it (**C**). Set the square aside.

(4) Using the metal ruler as your cutting guide, use the craft or utility knife to make a superficial cut directly into the cover following the outline of the square. *Note:* The incision should not be any deeper than 1⁄16 inch (1.6 mm). Cutting 1 mm deep would be ideal.

(5) Carefully peel the cut square from the book cover. It should reveal the book board underneath (**D**).

(6) Test the stamps on scrap paper. Use different colors for each terracotta pot and each of the plants. Select the combination of pot and plant you like the best. Use them to stamp the watercolor-paper square (**E**).

(7) Apply the PVA glue to the cover where you peeled away the square. Place the stamped watercolor square, and firmly press it down in place (**F**).

(8) Use the bone folder to smooth down the edges (**G**).

(9) Decorate the inside of your journal using the pot and plant stamps.

TIP: What a great gift for all your green-thumbed friends! But how about giving them a do-it-yourself kit? Make the journal with the decorated cover and then include a selection of small ink pads and carved stamps. That way, the recipient can create her own pages as she goes.

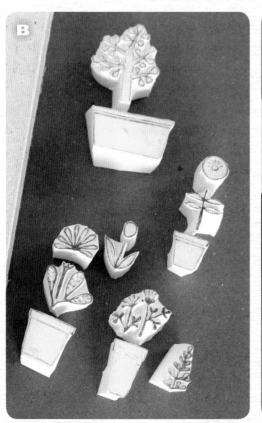

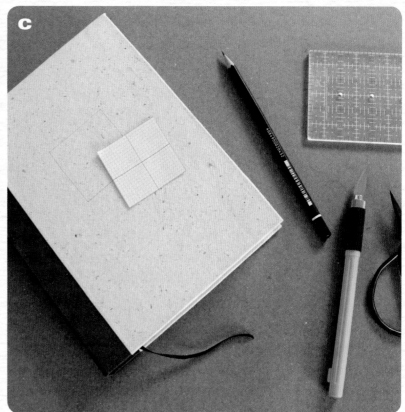

STAMPING on FABRIC

embroidered cactus tote

The subtle, graded shading on the cactus comes from inking the stamp in several colors. Embroidering the spines on the cactus lends the design authenticity along with adding visual texture.

what you'll need

- Tracing paper
- Soft-lead pencil
- Bone folder or small spoon
- Rubber carving blocks
- Linoleum cutter with No. 1 and No. 5 tips
- Craft knife or utility cutter
- Fabric ink pads in shades of blue and green and in purple, pink, and yellow
- Linen or cotton fabric in a neutral color
- Embroidery hoop
- Cotton embroidery floss in white, green, and violet
- Embroidery needle
- Cotton tote bag

what you do

1. Use the templates on page 130. Trace the cactus pieces using the soft-lead pencil. Use the bone folder or small spoon to transfer the images onto the rubber carving blocks (page 19).

2. Carve the stamps from the blocks using the linoleum cutter. Use the No. 1 cutter to carve the little flower details. Once you've carved the stamps, give them a light wash with warm water and a pH neutral soap, and let it air dry (**A**).

3. Practice inking the stamp to make a color gradient. First, ink the stamp with a base color. Then dab the stamp along the edges using complementary colors. To make the gradient uniform along the edges, dab several times without applying too much pressure. *Note:* On some of the cactus paddle pieces I added a little bit of purple and yellow to some of the edges.

A

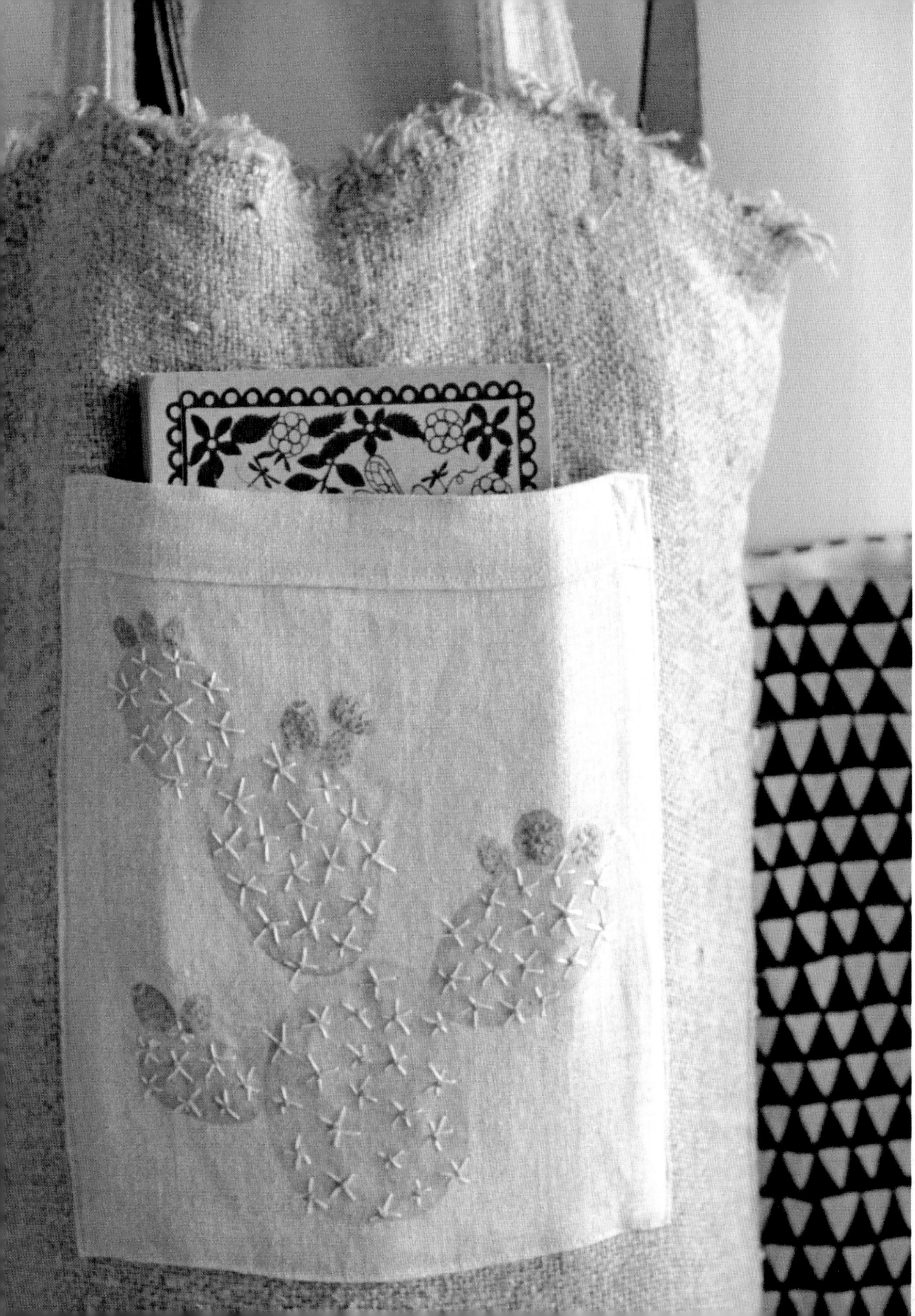

④ Test the stamps on scrap paper first, grouping the pieces to create a complete cactus using all the paddles, prickly pears, and blooms (**B**).

⑤ Once you're comfortable with your stamp design, go ahead and stamp on the piece of fabric.

⑥ Allow it to dry completely, and then follow the manufacturer's instructions for heat setting the ink. ***Note:*** When you heat set, make sure to iron the design on the reverse side of the fabric, placing a piece of scrap fabric underneath to prevent ruining your ironing board cover.

⑦ Place your stamped fabric in the embroidery hoop (**C**).

⑧ Use the white embroidery floss and needle to embroider the spines first using a long straight stitch, then make a French knot at the center of each spine cluster using the green floss (see Hand Stitches on page 29). For the prickly pear prickles, make tiny stitches using violet floss (**D**).

⑨ Turn the sides and bottom edge of the pocket in once, and press (**E**). Turn the top hem of the pocket under twice, and press. Use a sewing machine to sew the top hem of the pocket. Position and pin the pocket on the tote, and hand sew, using the slip stitch (page 29) to attach.

TIP: Sometimes inspiration stares you in the face. I didn't know what I'd do with this piece of embroidery until after I finished it. When I saw one of my market totes, I realized the embroidery would make a perfect pocket for holding my grocery-list notebook.

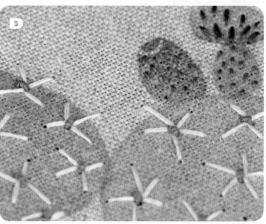

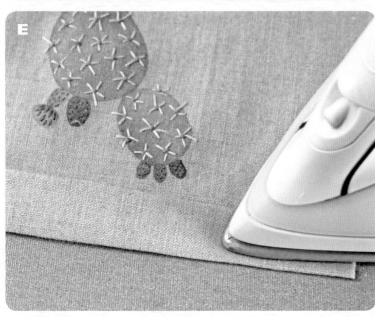

french press cozy

I love my French press, and I bet you love yours as well. This quilted cozy is beautiful, but also keeps the pot warm for enjoying those extra cups. The coffee plant, with its flowers and beans, is the natural inspiration for the design.

what you'll need

- Tracing paper
- Soft-lead pencil
- Bone folder or small spoon
- Rubber carving blocks
- Linoleum cutter with No. 1 and No. 5 tips
- Craft knife or utility cutter

- Piece of scrap paper
- Fabric ink pads in shades of green
- Fabric cat's-eye ink pad in red
- Cotton fabric in a neutral color, 2 pieces (big enough to fit most of the way around your press)

- Wool felt, 1 piece (slightly smaller than your cotton fabric pieces)
- Sewing machine
- Thread that matches the fabric
- Sisal or jute twine

what you do

① Use the templates on page 129. Trace the pieces using the soft-lead pencil. Use the bone folder or small spoon to transfer the images onto the rubber carving blocks (page 19) (**A**).

Note: You'll be making three separate stamps: one of the coffee plant with berries, another one of the flower, and a tiny stamp of the pistils of the flower.

2 Carve the stamps from the blocks using the linoleum cutter. Use the number 1 cutter to carve the little flower details. Once you've carved the stamps, give them a light wash with warm water and a pH neutral soap, and let them air dry.

3 Stamp the designs on the piece of scrap paper to test them out (**B**).

4 Prewash, dry, and iron your cotton fabric. The wool felt will be the batting layer in between the quilted cozy. *Note:* I used a vintage rice sack and incorporated the stamped number into my design.

5 Print the plant stamp first. When inking, use a basic green for the whole surface or use shades of green to create more depth. *Note:* I inked the stamp in one shade and then dabbed another shade on the outer edges of the leaves. Use the tip of the cat's-eye-shaped pad to dab a little bit of red onto the coffee berries.

6 Allow the ink to dry completely, and then follow the manufacturer's instructions for heat setting the ink. *Tip:* When you heat set, make sure to iron the design on the reverse side of the fabric, placing a piece of scrap fabric underneath to prevent ruining your ironing board cover.

7 Lay the two pieces of fabric with right sides together and sew around the edges, using the matching thread. Leave one of the edges open for turning. Turn the cozy, trim the seam allowances, and then slip the piece of wool felt inside between the layers. Close the opening by topstitching with the machine, or by hand using the slip stitch (page 29).

8 Machine quilt the three layers of fabric in parallel lines, using the foot of the sewing machine as a guide for spacing the stitching lines (**C**).

9 Use a zigzag stitch to attach one piece of sisal or jute twine to each side of the finished cozy. The twine will be used to close the cozy around your French press (**D**).

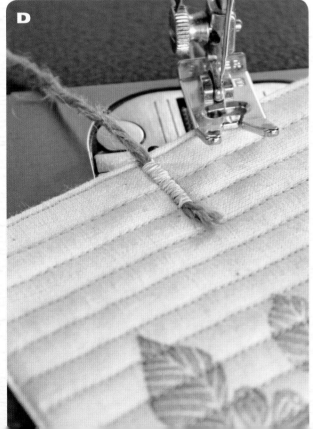

TIP: Hand wash the cozy in cold water when necessary, and hang to dry. When set correctly, the fabric inks will not run, but hand washing ensures the cute little tie won't fray.

bird brooch

Combining beads with stamping is a fabulous way to take advantage of two great craft mediums. After you embellish this beautiful little bird, just a bit of stuffing and a few stitches will complete your brooch.

what you'll need

- Tracing paper
- Soft-lead pencil
- Bone folder or small spoon
- Rubber carving block
- Linoleum cutter with No. 1 and No. 5 tips
- Craft knife or utility cutter

- Pigment ink pad in black
- Scrap paper
- Linen or cotton in a neutral color for the front
- Embroidery hoop
- Cotton thread
- Sewing needle

- Glass seed beads in colors of choice
- Embroidery floss
- Fabric in a complementary color for the back
- Polyester fiberfill or cotton stuffing
- Safety pin

what you do

(1) Use the template on page 129. Trace the bird design using the soft-lead pencil. Use the bone folder or small spoon to transfer the images onto the rubber carving block (page 19) (**A**).

(2) Carve the stamp from the block using the linoleum cutter. Use the number 1 cutter to carve the little details. Use the craft or utility knife to cut around the stamp to make a nice clean edge.

This is especially important when stamping on fabric. Once you've carved the stamp, give it a light wash with warm water and a pH neutral soap, and let it air dry (**B**).

③ Stamp the bird on the piece of scrap paper first to make sure the impression is even before you stamp it onto the fabric.

④ Stamp the bird onto the linen or cotton fabric. Allow it to dry completely (**C**), and then follow the manufacturer's instructions for heat setting the ink.

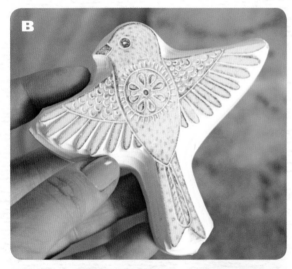

⑤ Place your stamped fabric in the embroidery hoop. Thread the sewing needle with the cotton thread, and knot the end. Insert the needle from the back of the fabric, slip a glass seed bead on the needle, and take a stitch to secure the bead (**D**). Repeat for each seed bead.

⑥ When you're done beading, you can use the embroidery floss to add embroidery stitches of your choosing. Use contrasting colors for even more detail (**E**).

⑦ Cut the beaded bird from the fabric leaving a 1-inch (2.5 cm) seam allowance all the way around it. Lay the bird on the complementary color of fabric, and use it as a pattern for cutting the back for the brooch (**F**).

⑧ Place the shapes with right sides together and all the edges aligned, and then pin. Use the needle and thread to hand stitch around the outline of the bird shape, leaving a small opening in the wing for turning and stuffing. Trim the seam allowance. To ensure smooth seams and no puckering, clip the concave curves and notch the convex curves (**G**). *Note:* To notch, cut small V-shaped wedges from the seam allowance; to clip, make small snips in the seam allowance.

⑨ Turn the bird inside out, and use the polyester fiberfill or cotton stuffing to stuff the shape. Use the slip stitch to sew the opening closed.

⑩ Stitch the safety pin on the back side of the brooch using the needle and the embroidery floss (**H**).

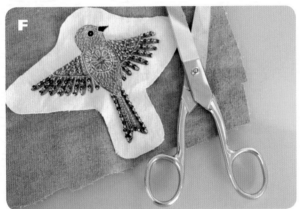

TIP: You can use any color of beads you desire to create your brooch. You may find it helpful to use colored pencils to sketch a few different color combinations first until you find one you like. You can also feature a special focal bead in the center of your design. Use the brooch to adorn your clothes or your favorite tote bag.

lake scene t-shirt

Make a scene to be seen. Create picturesque designs by combining smaller elements to make a whole. Any light-colored T-shirt will do when creating this tranquil image.

what you'll need

- Tracing paper
- Soft-lead pencil
- Bone folder or small spoon
- Rubber carving blocks

- Linoleum cutter with No. 1 and No. 5 tips
- Craft knife or utility cutter
- Fabric ink pads in colors of choice

- Scrap paper
- Kid's T-shirt in heather gray or any light color of choice
- Piece of cardboard

what you do

① Use the templates on page 131. Trace the pieces separately using the soft-lead pencil. Use the bone folder or small spoon to transfer the images onto the rubber carving blocks (page 19) (**A**).

② Carve the stamps from the blocks using the linoleum cutter. Use the number 1 cutter to carve the little details. Be sure to use the craft or utility knife to cut around the stamp to make a nice

A

clean edge. This is especially important when stamping on fabric. Once you've carved the stamps, give them a light wash with warm water and a pH neutral soap, and let it air dry (**B**).

③ Prewash the T-shirt and allow it to dry. Iron the shirt to create a very smooth work surface. Place a piece of cardboard inside the shirt to prevent any ink from bleeding through from the front to the back.

④ Test the stamps on scrap paper first, grouping the pieces to create the scene. Once you're satisfied with your design, begin stamping the T-shirt. Stamp the lake shape first and then the cattails and the three loons. Finish the scene by stamping the rocks and the moon (**C**).

⑤ Allow the inks to dry completely, and then follow the manufacturer's instructions for heat setting the ink. *Tip:* When you heat set, make sure to iron the design on the reverse side of the fabric, placing a piece of scrap fabric underneath to prevent ruining your ironing board cover.

B

TIP: Once you've created one scene, you can rearrange the elements to make another, or use the stamps individually or in different combinations for even more design potential.

three little birds pillow

Get ready to paint! The stamps themselves utilize simple shapes for making the impressions. But you'll add the details—the eyes, beaks, and feet—using black fabric paint.

what you'll need

- Tracing paper
- Soft-lead pencil
- Bone folder or small spoon
- Rubber carving blocks
- Linoleum cutter with No. 1 and No. 5 tips

- Craft knife or utility cutter
- Fabric ink pads in different colors and white
- Neutral color fabric, enough for the front and back of the pillow

- Black fabric paint
- Fine round brush
- Sewing machine
- Pillow insert

what you do

① Use the templates on page 132. Trace the designs using the soft-lead pencil, and then use the bone folder or small spoon to transfer the images onto the rubber carving blocks (page 19). You will have two bird bodies, two wings, and a tail.

② Carve the stamps from the rubber carving blocks using the linoleum cutter. Use the No. 1 tip to carve the lines in the wings and the tail. Once you've carved the stamps, give them a light wash with warm water and a pH neutral soap, and let them air dry (**A**).

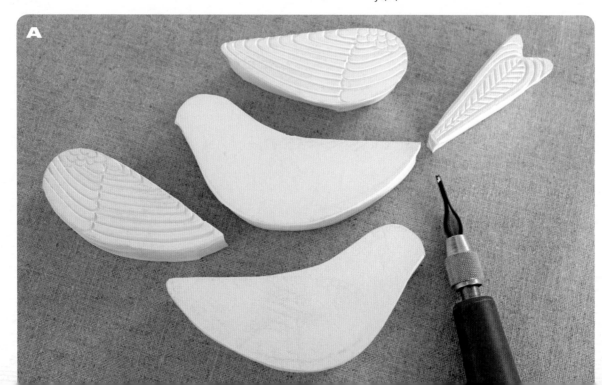

3 Test out the stamps on a scrap piece of fabric similar to the one you will be using for the pillow (**B**).

4 On the fabric for the front of the pillow, use a different color fabric ink to stamp each bird body. Alternate directions with one bird on top of the other; two will be facing right and one facing left (or vice versa). Use the white ink to stamp the wing on each bird. Use a contrasting color of ink for each of the tails. Allow the ink to dry completely (**C**).

5 Use black fabric paint with a very fine round brush to paint each of the bird's eyes, beaks, and feet. Paint the feet to make the birds look as if they're standing on top of each other. Let the paint dry for at least 20 minutes (**D**).

6 Follow the manufacturer's instructions for heat setting the ink. *Tip:* When you heat set, make sure to iron the design on the reverse side of the fabric, placing a piece of scrap fabric underneath to prevent ruining your ironing board cover.

7 Cut the fabric for the back of the pillow as wide as the front piece and slightly longer. Cut the back fabric into two rectangles, one slightly longer than the other. Hem one of the long edges on each rectangle.

8 Lay the stamped front on your work surface with the impression side facing up. Lay the rectangles with right sides down on the front, and pin all the way around. The hemmed edges will overlap to create an envelope back. Sew the front to the back, and turn right side out. Stuff the pillow with the pillow insert (**E**).

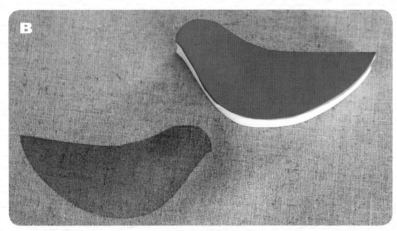

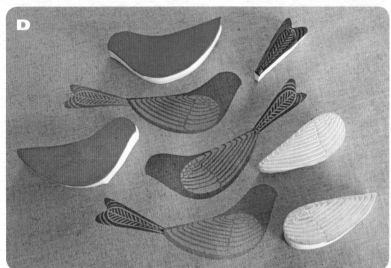

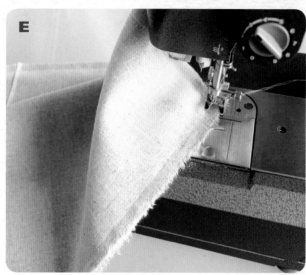

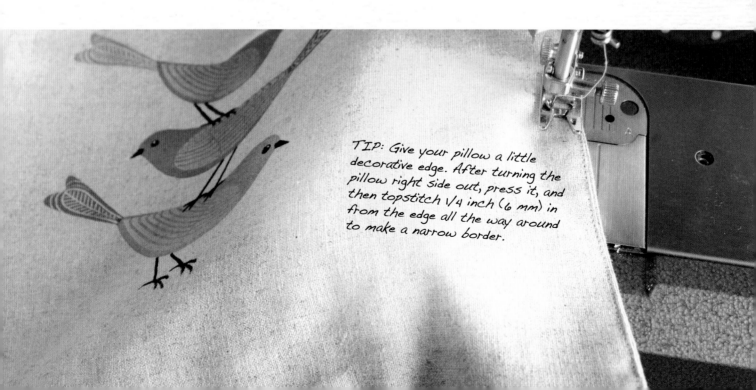

TIP: Give your pillow a little decorative edge. After turning the pillow right side out, press it, and then topstitch 1/4 inch (6 mm) in from the edge all the way around to make a narrow border.

STaMPinG
on
oTHer
surFaces

trinket box

Here's a different way to use a stamp. After carving, make an impression in polymer clay. Once baked, glue the plaque onto the lid of a small box, and paint it. You can adapt this technique to make larger designs, too.

what you'll need

- Tracing paper
- Soft-lead pencil
- Bone folder or small spoon
- Rubber carving block
- Linoleum cutter with No. 1 and No. 5 tips
- Craft knife or utility cutter
- White polymer clay
- Rolling pin or pasta machine used only for polymer clay
- Ruler
- Cardboard trinket box with lid, approximately 2 x 3 inches (5 x 7.6 cm)
- PVA glue
- Acrylic paint in a color of choice
- Medium flat brush

what you do

1 Use the template on page 129. Trace the design using the soft-lead pencil, and then use the bone folder or small spoon to transfer the image onto the rubber carving block (page 19) (**A**).

2 Carve the stamp from the rubber carving block using the linoleum cutter. Use the No. 1 tip to carve out the lines of the design, leaving the rest as negative space (page 23). Once you've carved the stamp, give it a light wash with warm water and a pH neutral soap, and let it air dry.

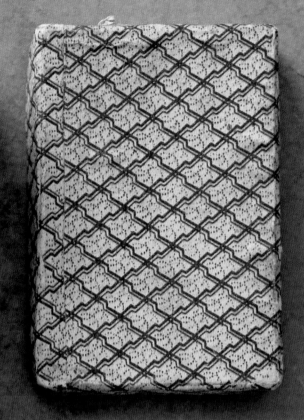

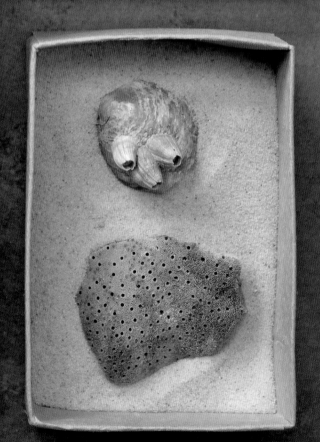

③ Knead a piece of the polymer clay until it is soft and pliable. Use a rolling pin or pasta machine to make a piece that's a little bigger than the size of the stamp and ⅛ inch (3 mm) thick (**B**). *Note:* Do not use utensils you use for food preparation for rolling out the polymer clay.

④ Use the stamp to make an impression in the polymer clay by applying a steady and uniform pressure. With the craft or utility knife, cut away any excess clay, leaving an edge around the impression. Use a ruler when cutting to make sure the edges are nice and straight (**C**).

⑤ Follow the manufacturer's instructions for baking the clay. Allow to cool completely.

⑥ Use the PVA glue to glue the polymer clay piece to the lid of the cardboard trinket box. Allow to dry.

⑦ Paint the lid using the acrylic paint and medium flat brush. *Note:* I chose to paint the edge a shade darker than the top piece. Allow to dry.

c

TIP: Trinket boxes mostly hold small treasures, but there's no limit to the size box you can embellish. Just create stamps that are bigger to match the size of your box lid. In fact, why not make a box big enough to hold your favorite stamps?

terracotta pots

Though I find terracotta pots beautiful as is, I couldn't help making them sing with a bit of easy stamping. The gradient effect of the ink fading away gives the pots a weathered look.

what you'll need

- Tracing paper
- Soft-lead pencil
- Bone folder or small spoon
- Rubber carving block

- Linoleum cutter with No. 1 and No. 5 tips
- Craft knife or utility cutter
- Pigment ink pads in black and white

- Scrap paper
- 2 small terracotta pots
- Small towel

what you do

① Use the template on page 130. Trace the design using the soft-lead pencil, and then use the bone folder or small spoon to transfer the image onto the rubber carving block (page 19).

② Carve the stamp from the rubber carving block using the linoleum cutter (**A**). Use the No. 1 tip when carving out tiny nooks and crannies, such as the tips of the triangle (**B**). Once you've carved the stamp, give it a light wash with warm water and a pH neutral soap, and let it air dry.

3　When inking a bigger stamp like this one, lay the stamp on the table or work surface with the carved side up, then hold the stamp firmly with your left hand while you ink it with the ink pad facing down. Pat the pad repeatedly with an even pressure to completely cover the surface of the stamp. Test out the stamp on a piece of scrap paper (**C**).

4　Make sure your terracotta pots are clean and dry. To prevent the pot from slipping as you stamp, fold the small towel and lay the pot on its side on top of it. Bend the inked stamp to match the curvature of the pot, and apply an even and steady pressure when making the impression. Begin stamping from the rim of the pot and work your way toward the bottom (**D**).

(5) Without reinking the stamp, make another impression just below the first one to create the gradient effect. Repeat until the stamp has no ink left on it. You may find it helpful to practice making this effect beforehand on a piece of scrap paper. To cover the whole surface of the pot, repeat around the perimeter of the container. Allow to dry.

(6) You can also decorate only the rim of a pot by stamping all around it. Just make sure you align the stamp for continuity around the rim. Allow the ink to dry before use (**E**).

109

TIP: I love keeping pots of fresh herbs on my windowsill or by my kitchen door. It takes nothing to snip a few leaves when I'm cooking, and the aroma from the fresh-cut herbs fills the air.

pretty stone

Instead of making one large stamp, make a few small stamps that you can combine in different ways. Working this way gives you the versatility to customize the pattern to the shape of the object you're stamping. You can also use this technique to build a larger motif from several smaller ones.

111

what you'll need

- Tracing paper
- Soft-lead pencil
- Bone folder or small spoon
- Rubber carving block
- Linoleum cutter with No. 1 and No. 5 tips
- Craft knife or utility cutter
- Ink pad in white
- Scrap paper
- Medium-sized smooth river rock or beach stone
- Red acrylic paint
- Small round brush

what you do

1. Use the templates on page 131. Trace the designs using the soft-lead pencil, and then use the bone folder or small spoon to transfer the image onto the rubber carving block (page 19) (**A**).

2. Carve the stamps in the rubber carving block using the linoleum cutter (**B**).

3. If you carved two motifs on the same block, cut them apart to make two separate stamps. Then give them a light wash with warm water and a pH neutral soap, and let them air dry (**C**).

4. Ink the stamps and test them on the scrap paper. Practice making a repeat pattern with the leaves (**D**).

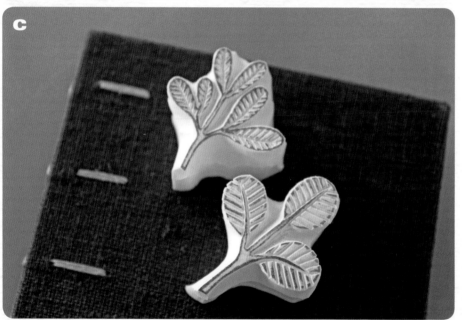

5. Wash the stone well. Use a brush and a little bit of pH neutral soap to scrub off any loose dirt or sand, rinse well, and allow it to dry completely.

6. Ink the stamp and make your impressions on the stone. Since stones have a curved surface, you will need to apply pressure to the stamp while bending it. Make sure the stone doesn't move out of place. If it does shift a little, you'll end up with a blurry impression. You might find it helpful to practice on an extra stone first.

7. You can use one of the single leaf designs to make an impression on a smaller stone. *Note:* Lighter rocks also look great when you make the impression using black ink (**E**).

8. Once you've repeated your stamp to form a bigger branch, use the small round brush to add little dots of red to create berries (**F**).

TIP: Use your decorated stone as a paperweight, to decorate a flowerpot, or simply put it on a windowsill as a natural decoration. I have several in my studio that I use as paperweights because I like to work with the windows open, and it often gets very windy!

wall stamp border

Love the look of stenciling but don't like all the fuss of paints and brushes—not to mention the frustrating smears that appear when moving the stencil? Try stamping your design instead. It's a quick and easy way to decorate a room in no time.

what you'll need

- Tracing paper
- Soft-lead pencil
- Bone folder or small spoon

- Rubber carving blocks, one at least 4 x 6 inches (10.2 x 15.2 cm)
- Linoleum cutter with No. 1, No. 2, and No. 5 tips

- Craft knife or utility cutter
- Ink pads in two contrasting colors
- Scrap paper

what you do

① Use the templates on page 133. Trace the stencil design using the soft-lead pencil and tracing paper. *Tip:* Tape the tracing paper design to the area you wish to stencil to make sure you're happy with its size. If you're making a border around a window or doorway, plan out how to space the design (**A**). Adjust the design size if necessary.

② Use the bone folder or small spoon to transfer the larger image onto the 4 x 6-inch (10.2 x 15.2 cm) rubber carving block (page 19). Use smaller blocks or white erasers when transferring the flower and single leaf (**B**).

116

3. Carve the stamps from the blocks using the linoleum cutter (**C**). Use the No. 1 and No. 2 tips for the lines, and the No. 5 tip and craft or utility knife for carving out all the excess rubber. Once you've carved the stamps, give them a light wash with warm water and a pH neutral soap, and let them air dry.

4. Test out the stamps on the scrap paper using the ink pad colors you'll be using for the wall. You'll be using three stamps: leaves on a stem, a single leaf, and the flower. You'll use the single leaf to complete the ends of the stenciled border (**D**).

5. Make sure the wall is clean and dry before stamping. Use the edge of the window frame as your guide, leaving 1½ inches (3.8 cm) between the stamped image and the edge of the frame.

6. Stamp the leaves first and then the flower (**E**). Use the single leaf to complete the ends. To avoid smearing the design, allow the ink to dry at least 24 hours before touching it.

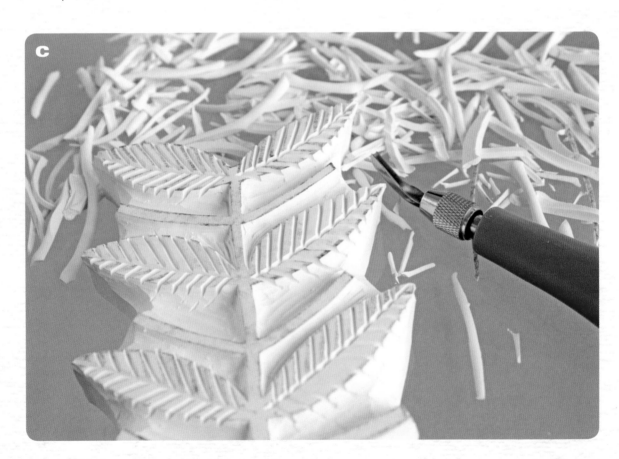

c

D

E

TIP: Use the stamps to create a variety of stenciled looks. Stamp around any window, door, or mirror to create a decorative border. Stencil the walls of a room at the top just under the crown molding. You can also use the stamps to make one or more accent motifs in the bathroom or kitchen.

MOtiFS

If you'd like to swap out a design that was used in a project, here are some additional motifs you might want to try.

THIS BOOK IS GREAT

AIR MAIL

tempLates

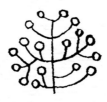

Eraser Stamps
page 34

Gift Tag
page 38

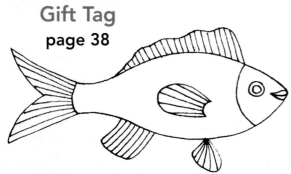

Accordion Journal
page 60

EX LIBRIS

Bookplate
page 44

Embroidered Cards
page 65

**Butterfly
Vintage Postcard**
page 70

Photo Frame
page 52

Stationery
page 41

Wrapping Paper
page 48

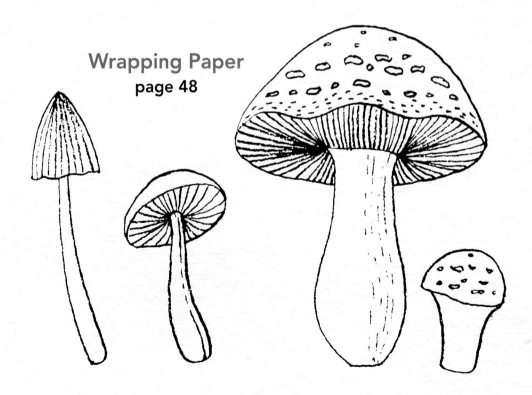

Bird Brooch
page 88

French Press Cozy
page 84

Trinket Box
page 102

Terracotta Pots
page 106

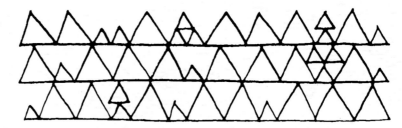

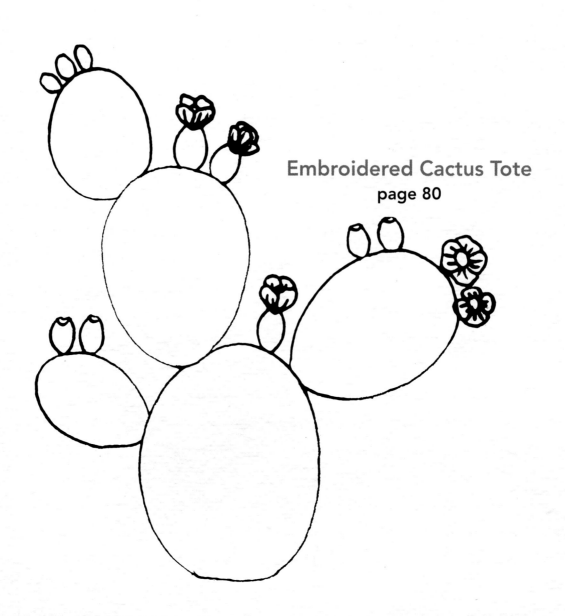

Embroidered Cactus Tote
page 80

Lake Scene T-Shirt
page 92

Pretty Stone
page 111

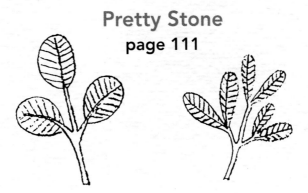

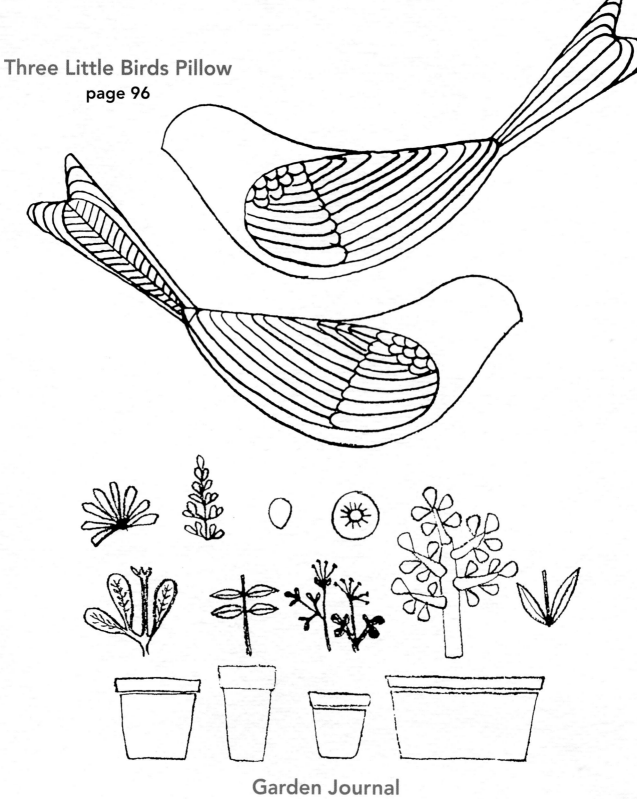

Three Little Birds Pillow
page 96

Garden Journal
page 74

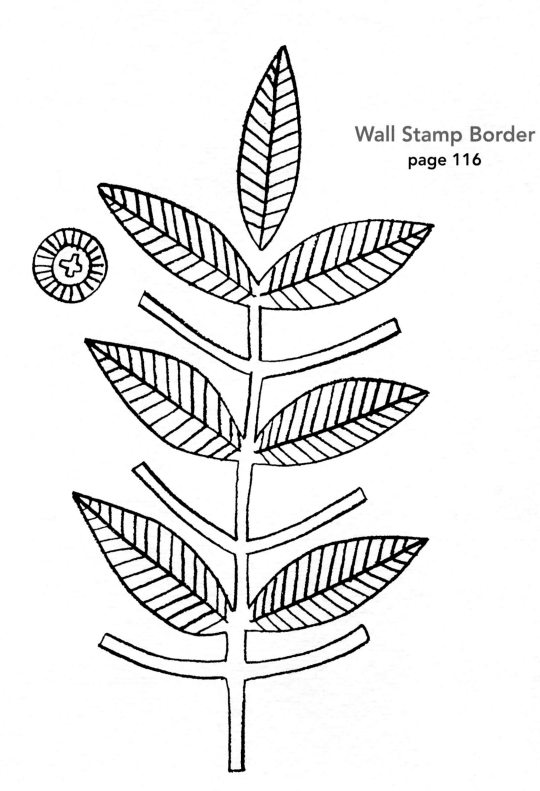

Wall Stamp Border
page 116

acknowledgments

To the Lord my God, for allowing me to do what I love.

To my mom and dad, for all their encouragement and love.

To Manolo, my best friend and love of my life, for always having my back.

To my beautiful sons Israel and Daniel, for being my constant inspiration and motivation.

To my brother Sergio, and my sisters: Karyn, Becki, and Moni, for being my biggest fans.

To my sweet friends: Margie, Sonia, Arounna, and Julia for their support and inspiration.

To Bookhou.com for all the beautiful printed fabrics that appear in the background of some of my projects.

To my wonderful editor, Linda Kopp, for making this process such an enjoyable one.

To Lark Crafts, for the opportunity to make a beautiful book.

To all my amazing blog followers and their constant support of my art.

Without each one of you this book would not be possible.

ABOUT THE AUTHOR

Geninne D. Zlatkis

Geninne is an artist, illustrator, and graphic designer living outside Mexico City with her husband Manolo, their two very creative boys, and a cute border collie named Turbo. She was born in New York, but shortly after, her parents began traveling around South America, where she lived in seven different countries and went to several English-speaking schools.

Her love for arts and crafts began at a very early age; her mom says she started drawing when she was two years old, and it continued to be her favorite activity through her childhood and teenage years. By the time she decided what to study in college she was 100 percent sure it had to be in the visual arts. Geninne studied architecture in Chile for a couple of years before graduating as a graphic artist in Mexico.

She works in a variety of media including watercolor, ink, and pencil. She sews, embroiders, and loves to hand-carve rubber stamps, selling prints of her watercolors at her online Etsy Shop geninne.etsy.com. Geninne loves birds and flowers and has been taking photos since she was 15 years old. Her inspiration comes primarily from nature; it is the driving force of her work. She never took a watercolor class, which helped her develop her own style of painting. Visit her blog at www.geninne.com.

index